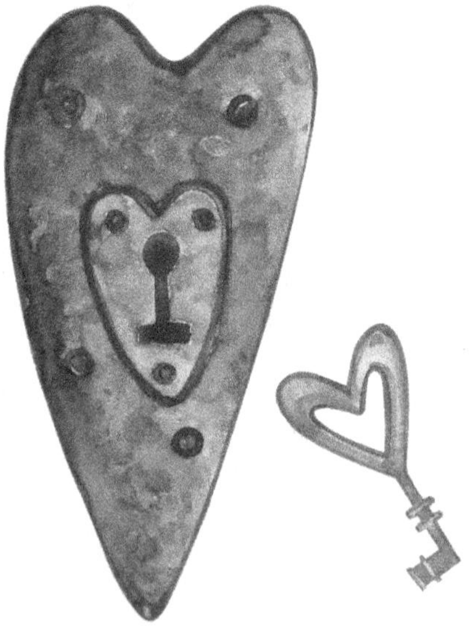

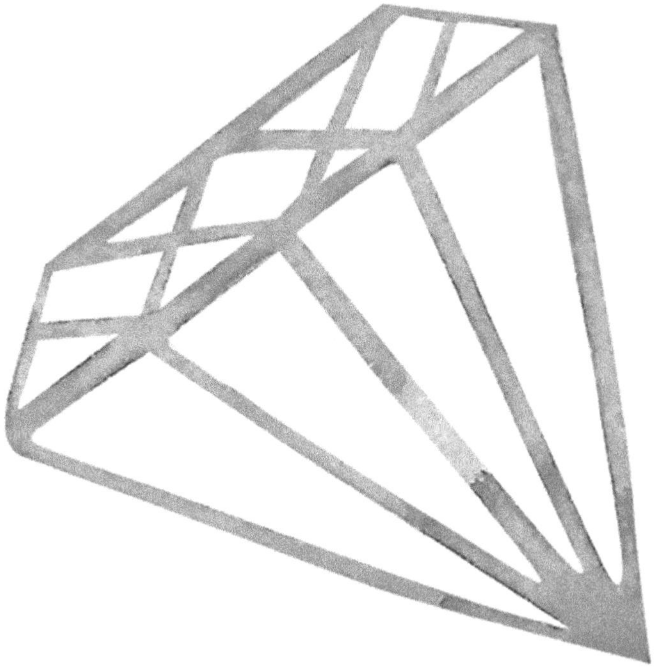

you
+
me
=
love

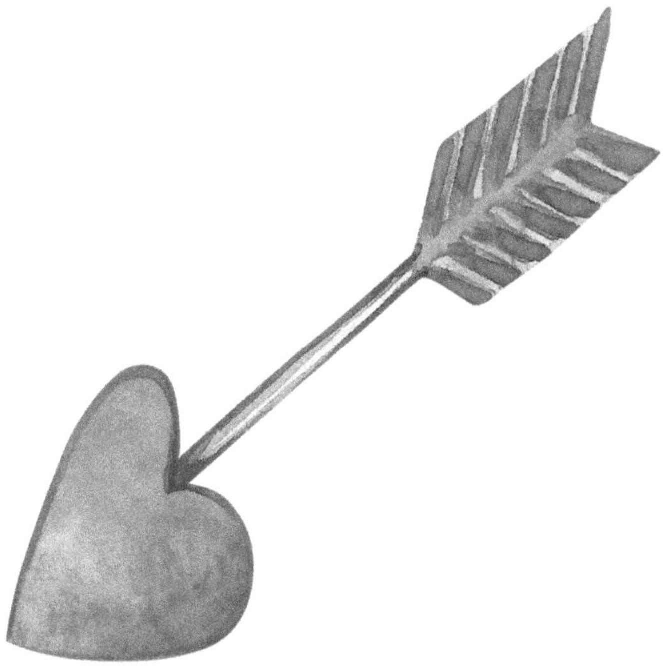

i love you

Love you

LO
VE

you are loved

love is all you need

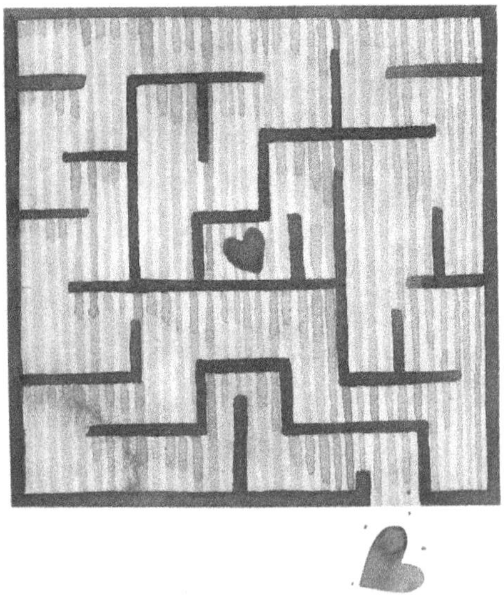

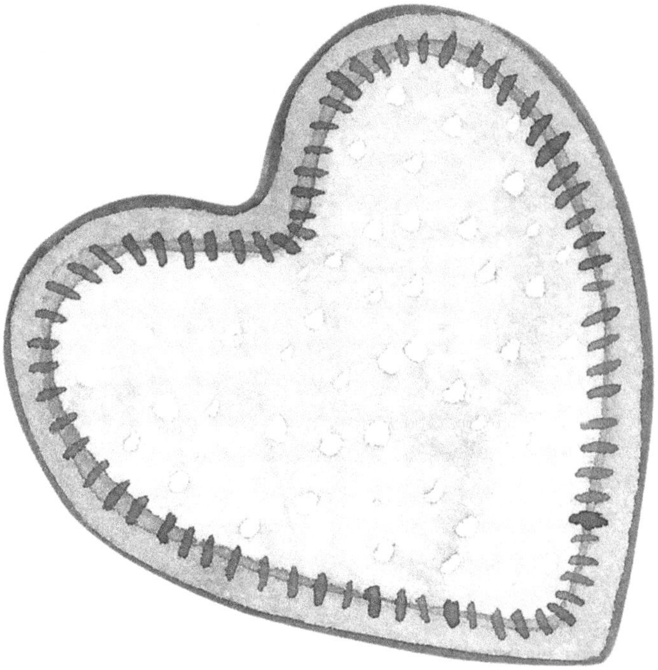

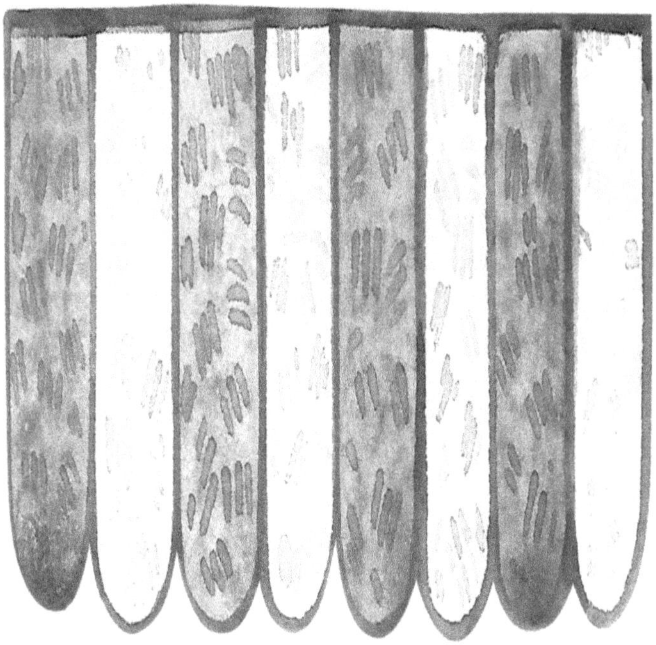

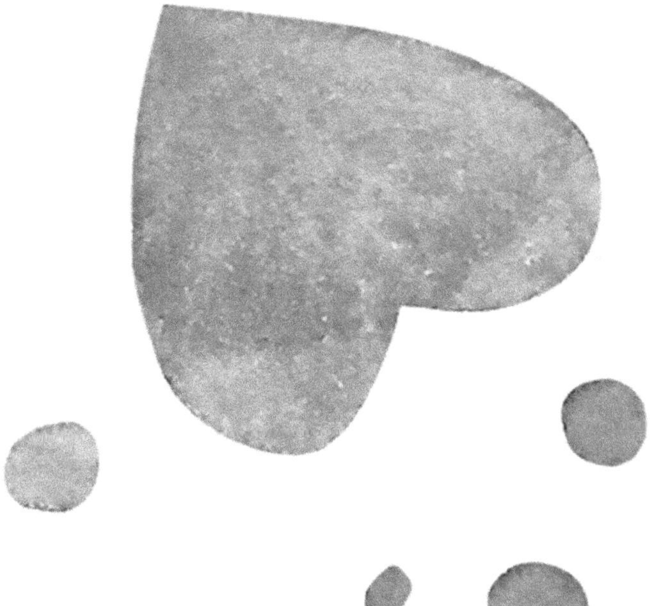

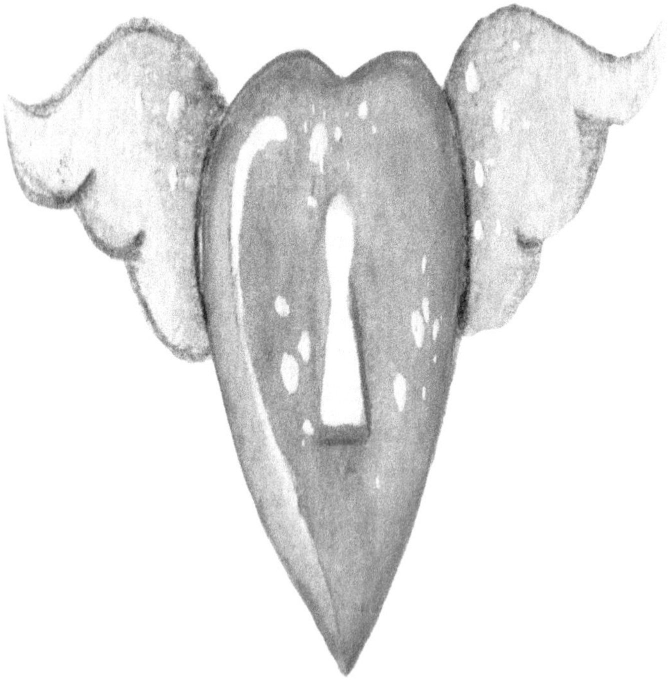

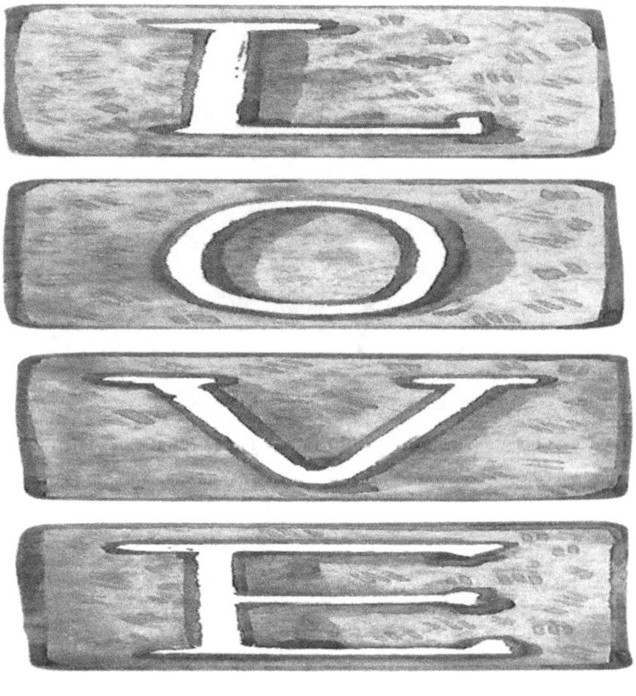
L
O
V
E

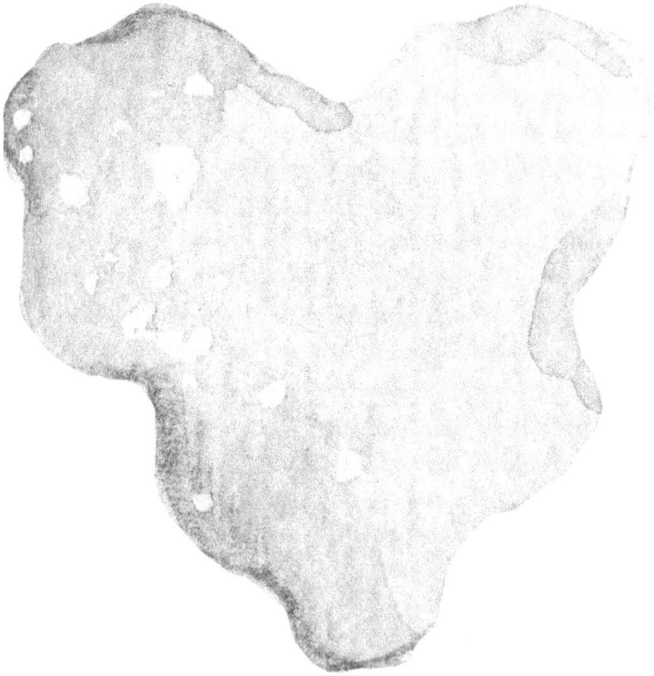

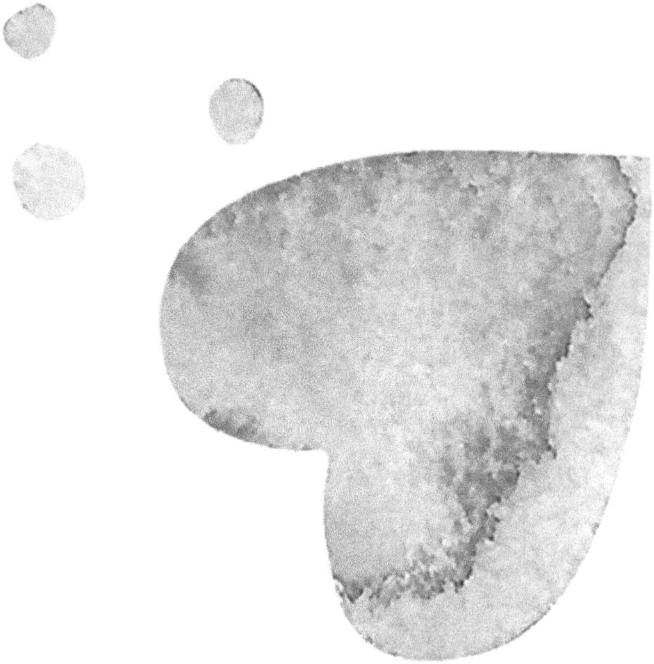

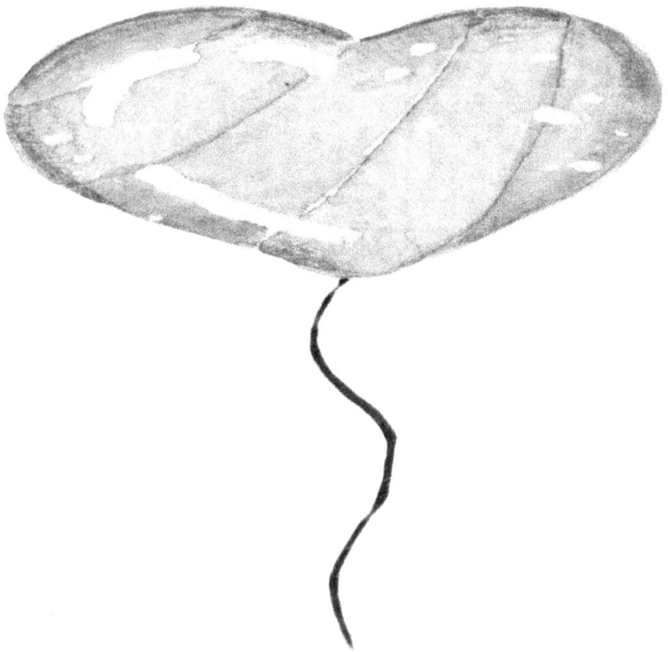

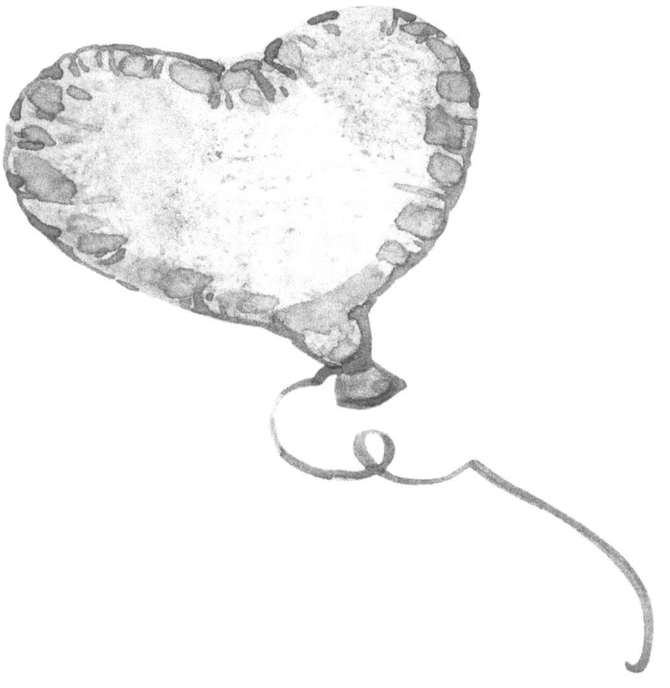

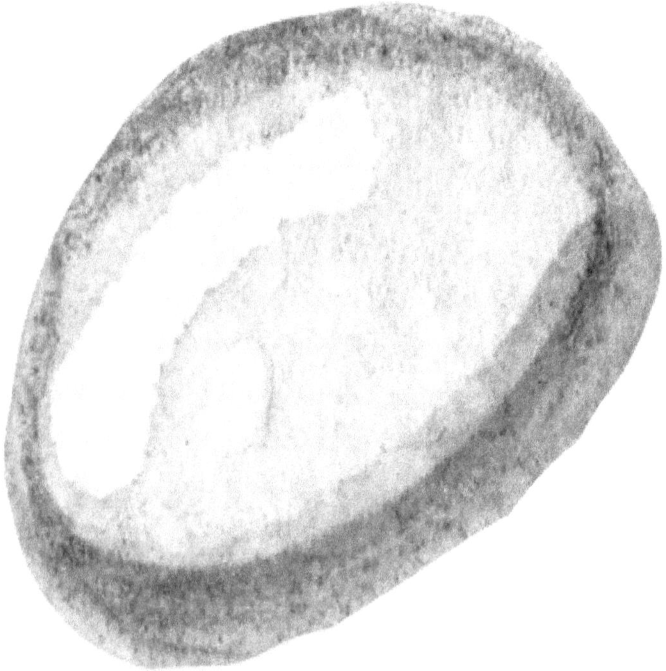

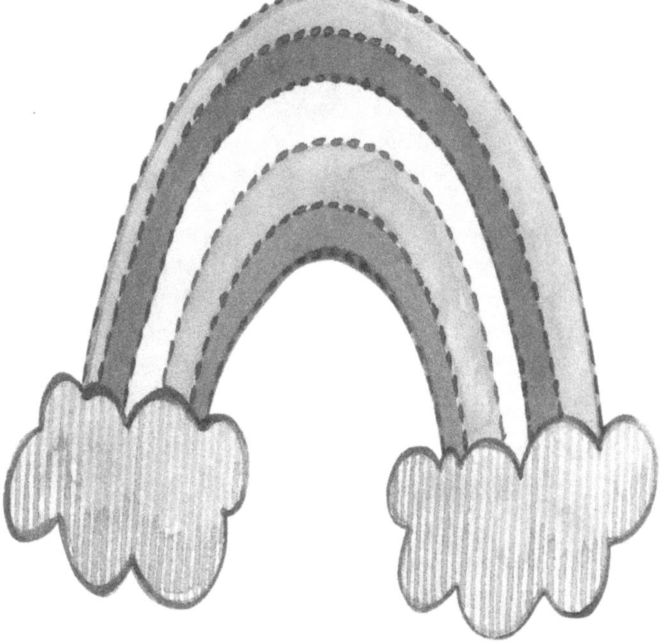

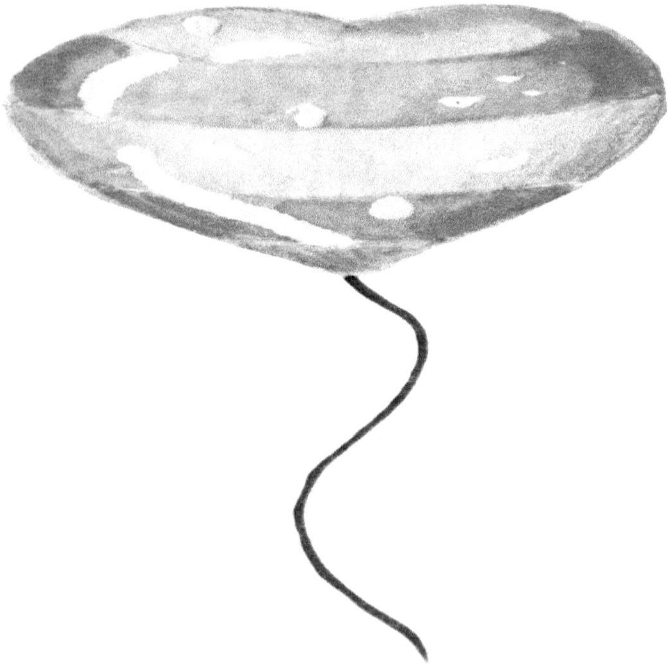

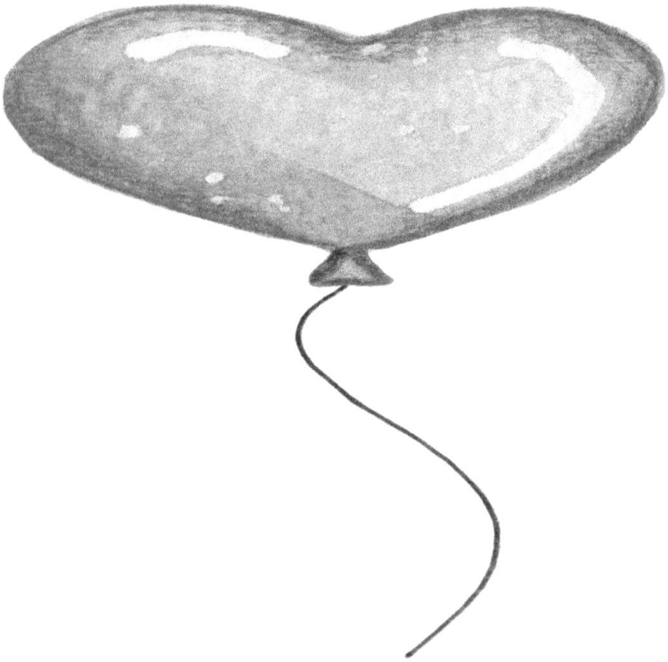

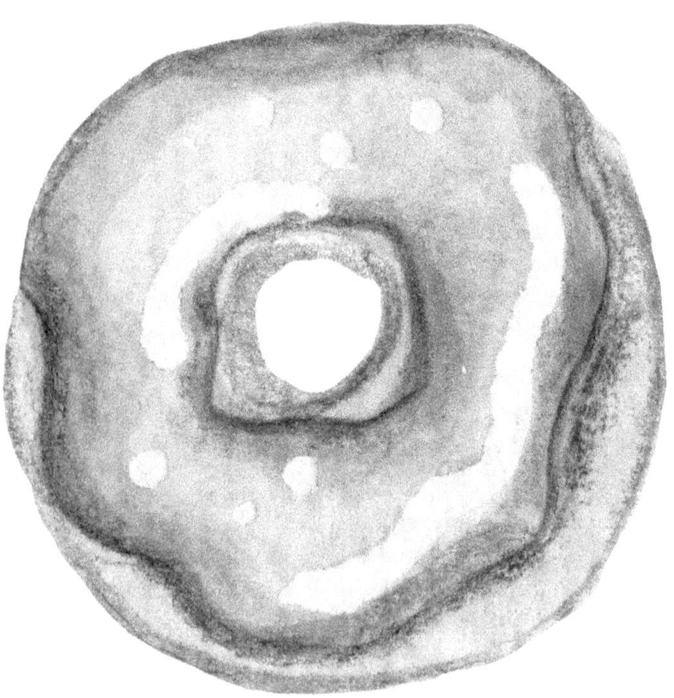

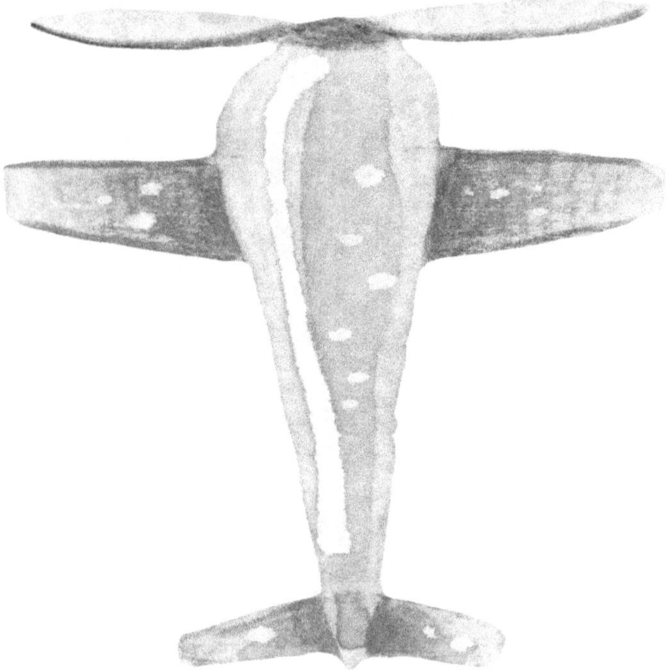

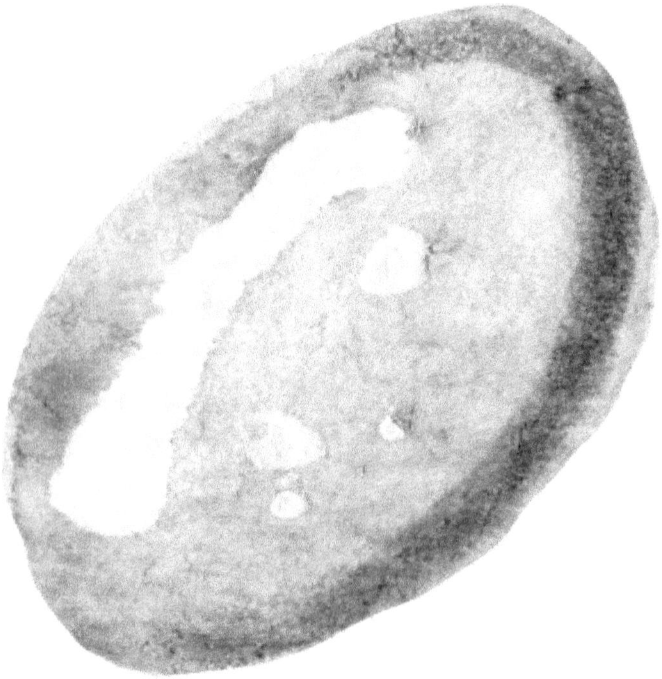

love

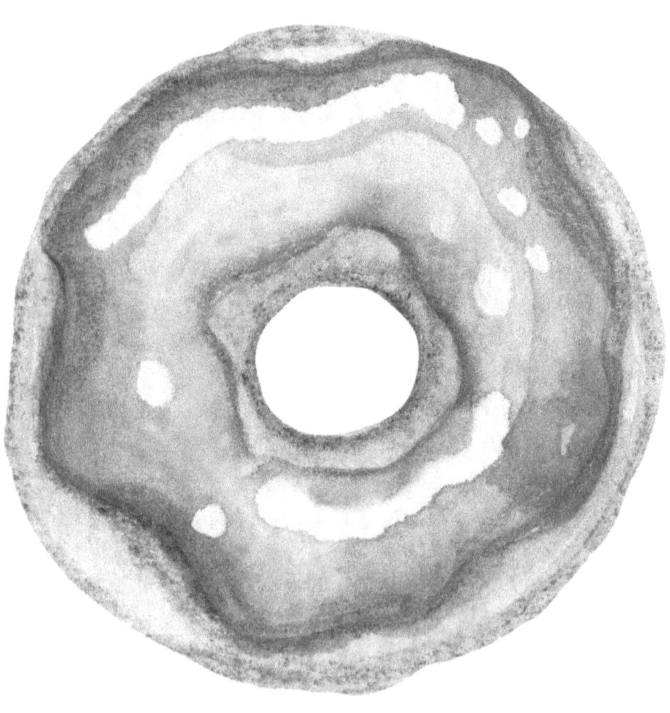

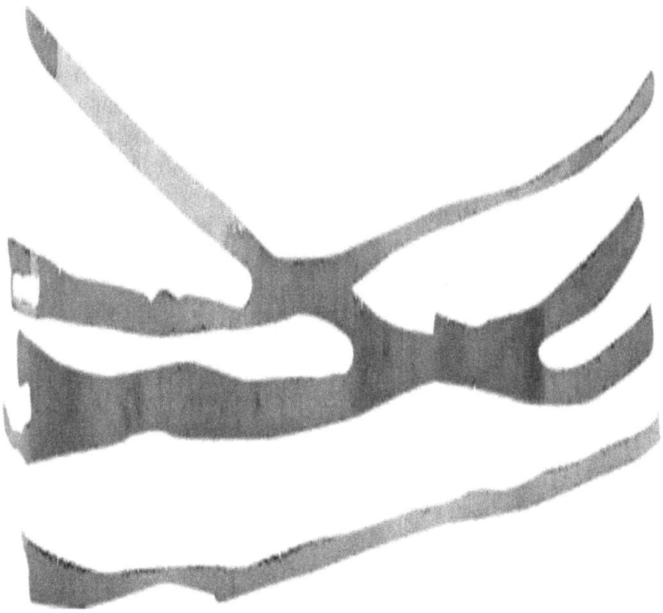

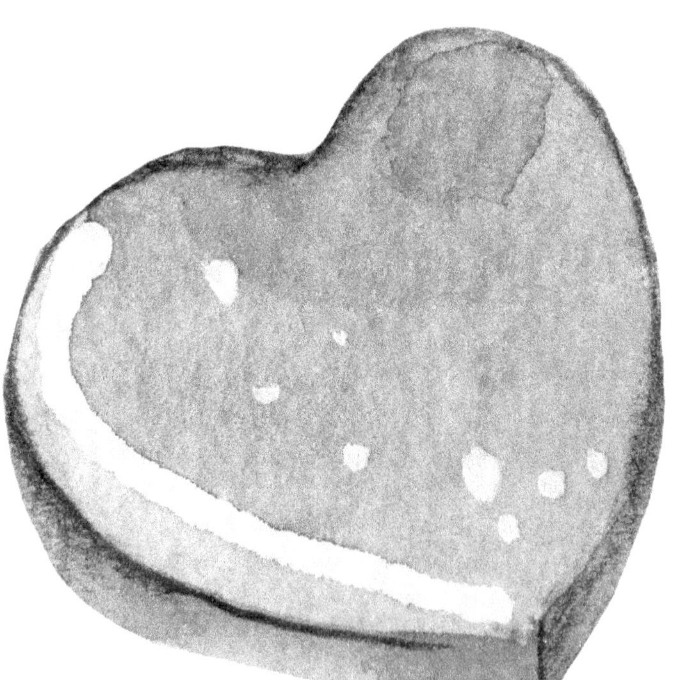

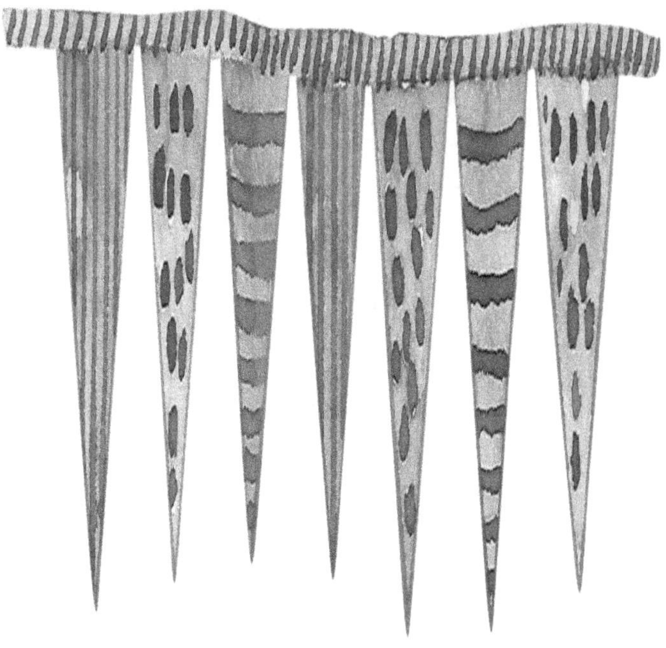

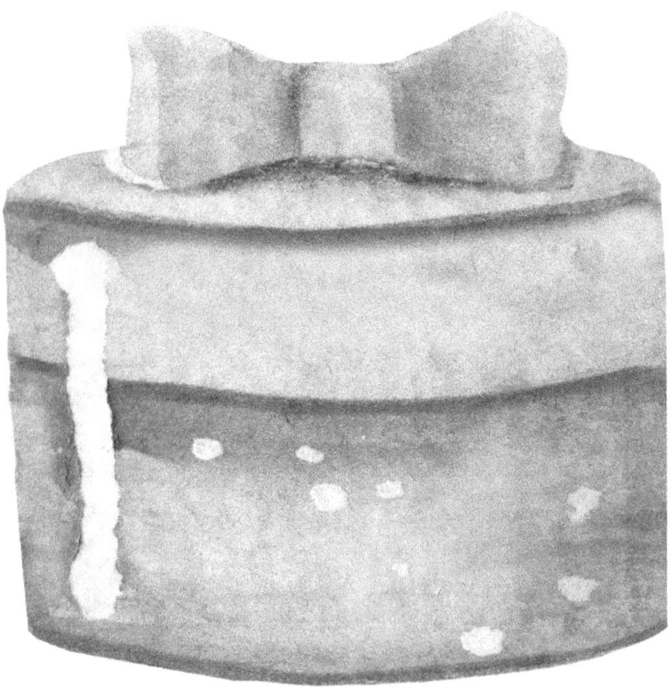

YAY

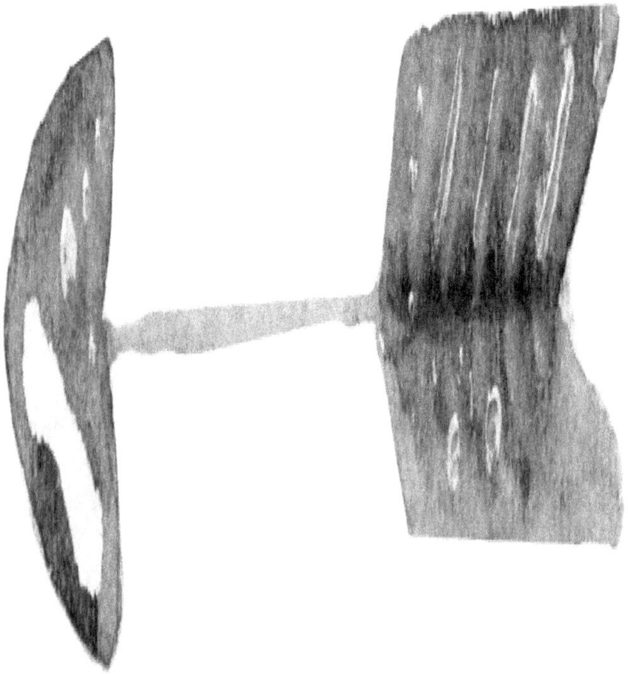

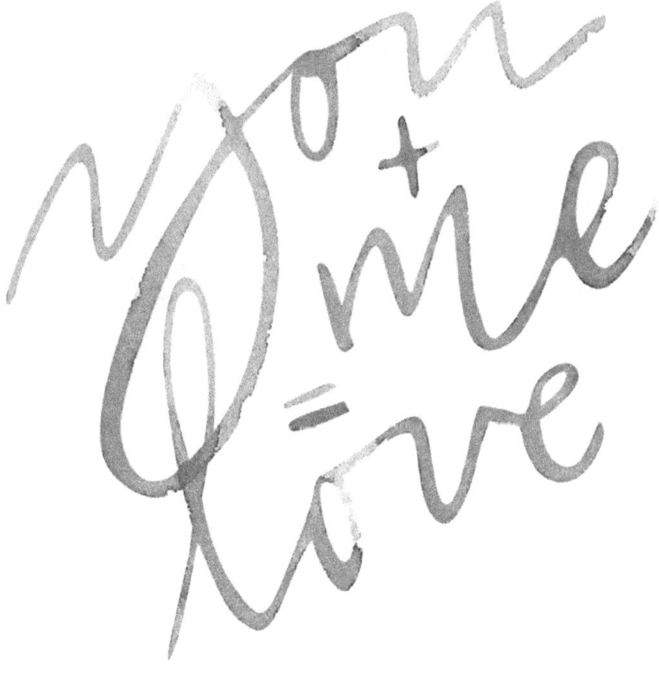
you
+
me
=
love

believe
IN
Love

love

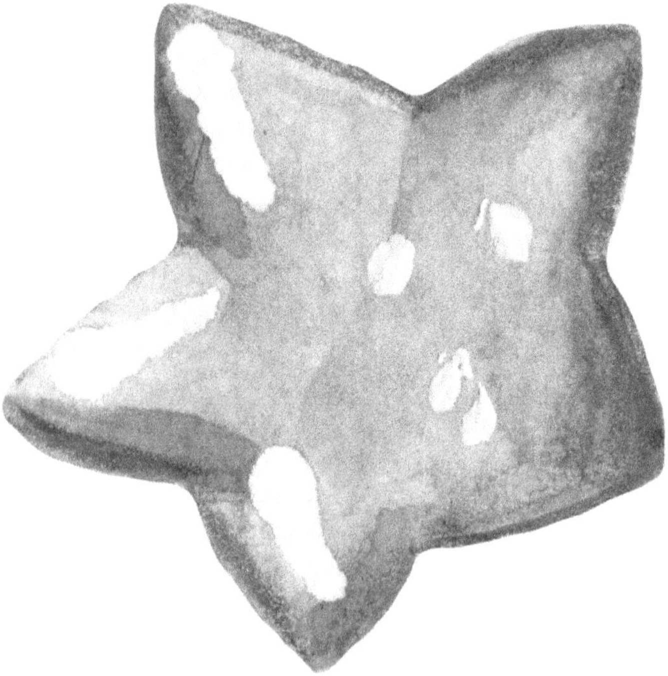

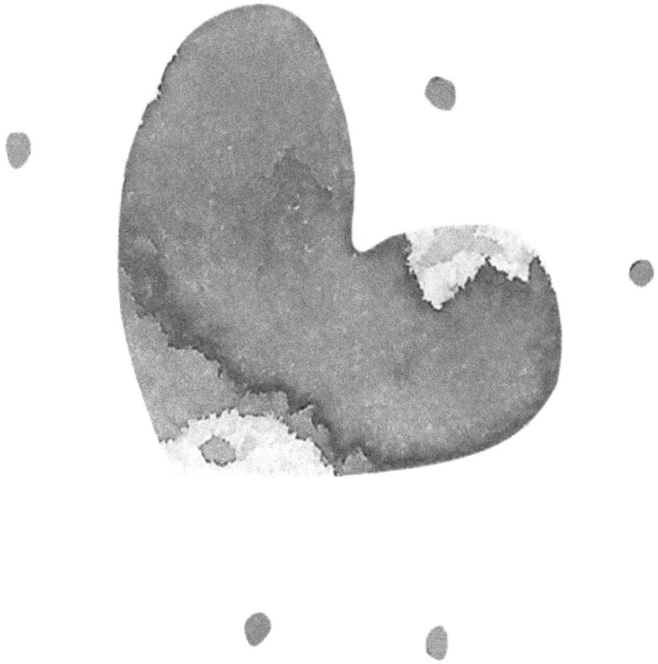

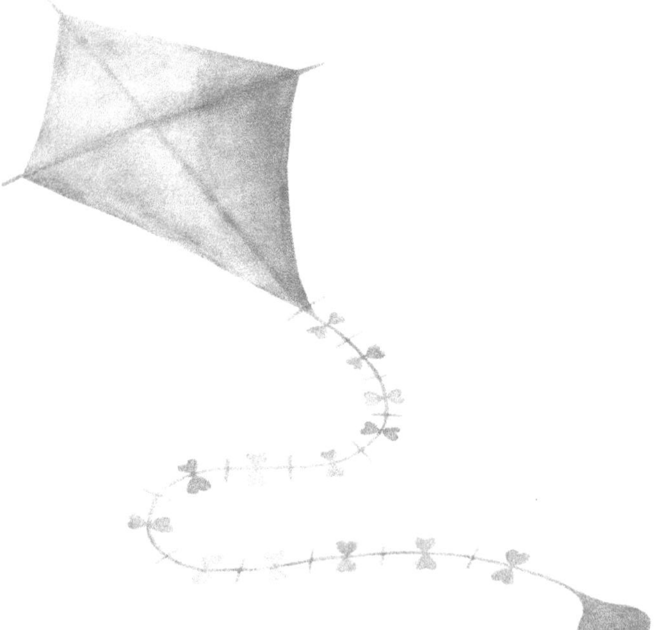

i love you

love you

LOVE

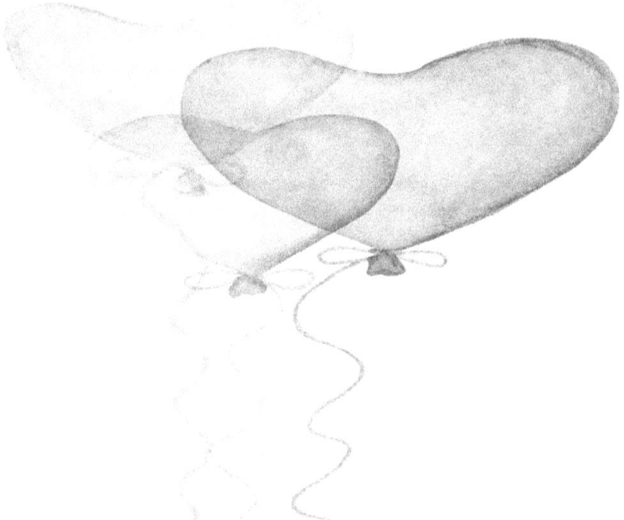

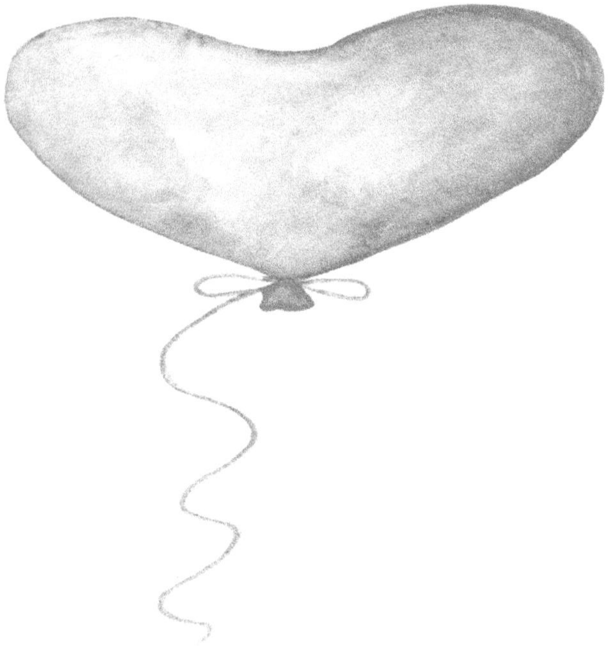

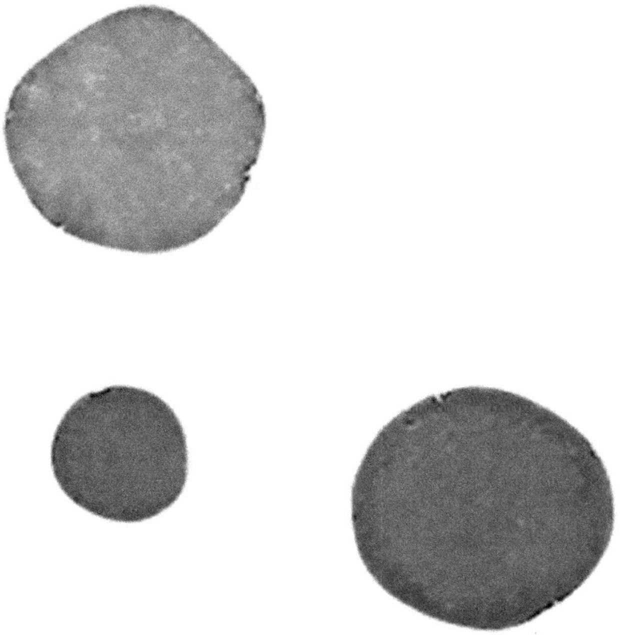

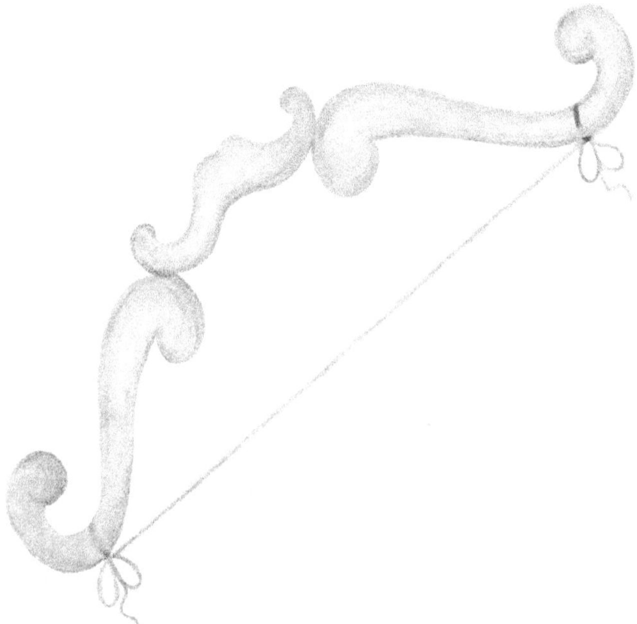

you are loved

love is all you need

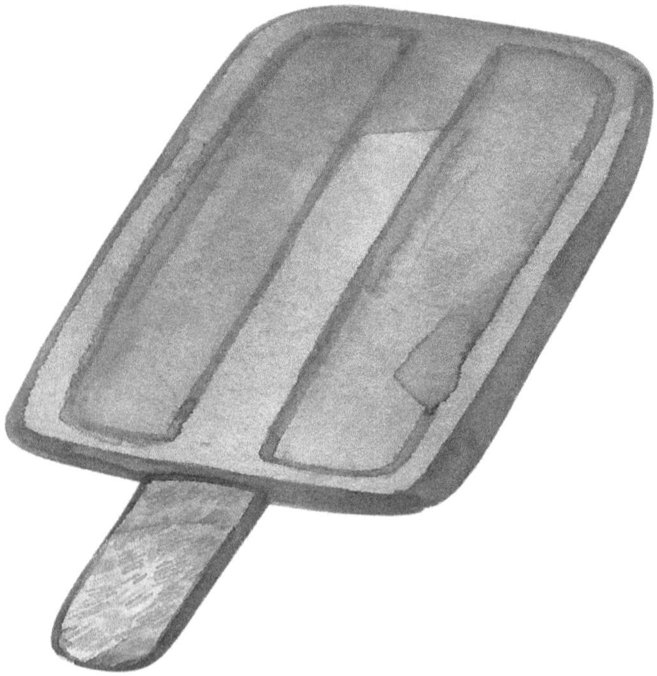

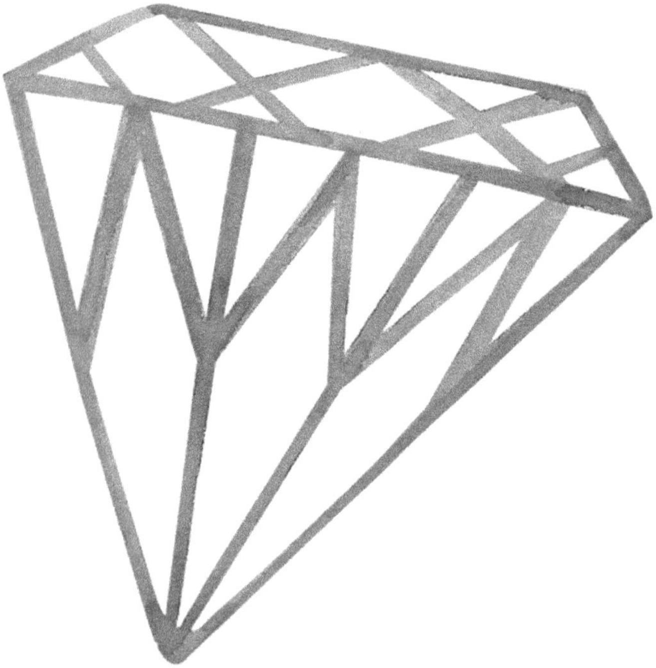

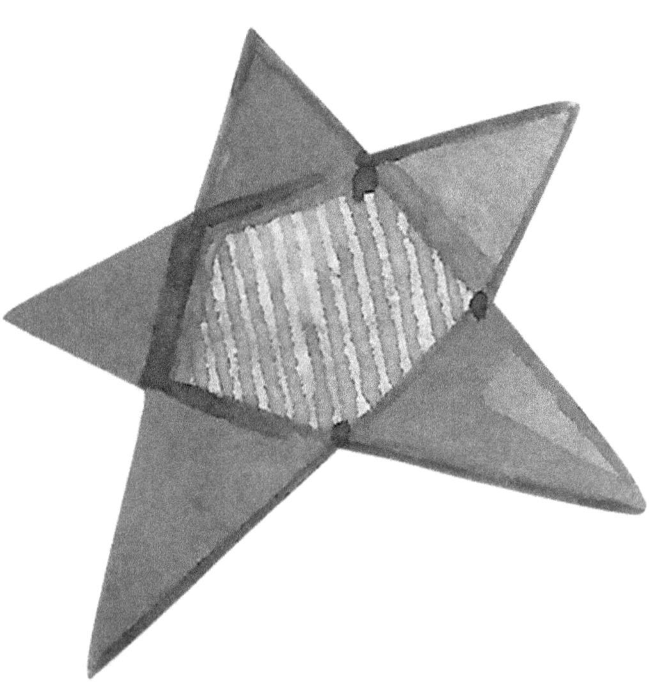

LOVE

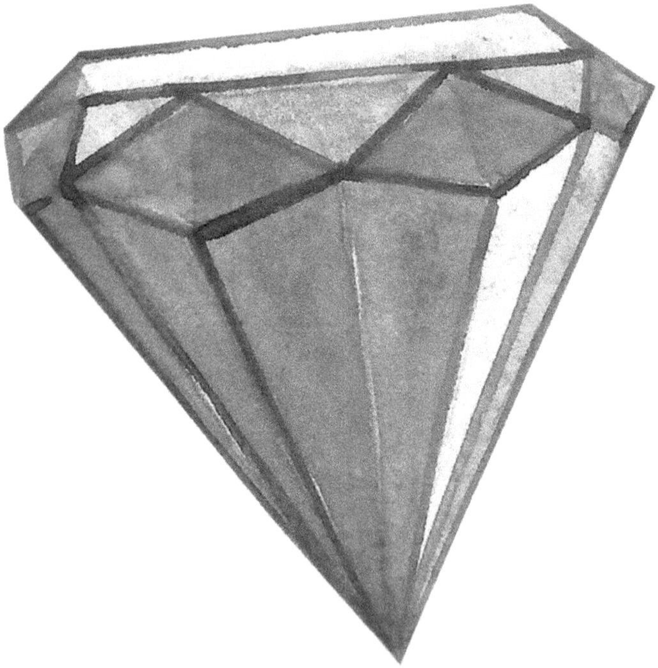

- Acts of Kindness Tracker -

- Acts of Kindness Tracker -

- Acts of Kindness Tracker -

Notes

Notes

Notes

www.ingramcontent.com/pod-product-compliance
Lightning Source LLC
LaVergne TN
LVHW060139080526
838202LV00049B/4025
* 9 7 8 3 3 4 7 0 2 9 9 6 5 *